THE CINEPHILE POEMS

Alan Price was born in Liverpool and now lives in London. He's a poet, scriptwriter, short story writer, book reviewer, film critic for the online *London Grip* and *Magonia*. His TV film *A Box of Swan* was broadcast on BBC 2. Alan has scripted five short films that have won film festival awards and commendations. His debut collection of poetry *Outfoxing Hyenas* was published by Indigo Dreams in 2012. This was followed by several other pamphlets and collections. Alan is presently writing fiction and has completed a novel and two collections of short stories awaiting publication.

By the Same Author

Poetry

Outfoxing Hyenas
Angels at the Edge
Mahler's Hut
Wardrobe Blues for a Japanese Lady
Restless Voices
Bewilderment
(with paintings by Herve Constant)

Fiction
The Other Side of the Mirror
The Illiterate Ghost

THE CINEPHILE POEMS

Alan Price

The High Window

First published in the UK in 2022 by The High Window Press
3 Grovely Close
Peatmoor
Swindon SN5 5DN
Email: abbeygatebooks@yahoo.co.uk

ISBN: 9798370682971

Designed and typeset in Palatino Linotype by The High Window Press.

INTRODUCTION

We live in an age of the blogger and internet lists. The 100 best films, novels, paintings, songs, poems, etc. Of course list-compiling long predates the internet. And as for film bests, Sight and Sound magazine began its international poll in 1952. This is still a regular feature every 10 years. Their criteria would be serious artistic content – films that were cinematic landmarks and/or had great humanistic and popular appeal. Back in the late 50s cinema was seen to matter in so far as it could be classified as Film Art (an unhelpful term as it suggested that cinema needed to prove that it was capable of being considered the 7th major art form.) Poll critics, then and now provide a paragraph or two explaining why a film is important and why it personally matters to them.

So, what docs this have to do with the 'art' of poetry? Perhaps nothing. Maybe everything. I remember watching a TV documentary on classical music where the pianist Alfred Brendel said something to the effect that the highest compliment you could make about a work of art was to call it poetic. That this was the summit of artistic depth. Beethoven and Shakespeare certainly had it. But did jazz, popular music and the movies give you real poetry – that frisson of pleasure providing deep insight to change your life a little?

Many of the films, in my contents list for *The Cinephile Poems* achieve this aim. A few films don't have such pretensions to greatness but they are still films that I love. Yet all manage to convey an epiphany. They woke me up to perceive the world in a different light. And I wanted to convey, through the prose poem, the insight I had on my first and subsequent viewings. (The only exception being was to include one truly bad movie *Mesa of Lost Women* where trash triumphed over art.)

Undertaking to write *The Cinephile Poems* I felt it best to drop the distinction between art-film versus entertainment-film. The more I wrote the more I wanted to illustrate their mark on my personal history. It was very hard to ration my choice of films to 39 poems as hundreds, even thousands, of films have affected me for good or ill – as Woody Allen once said that he couldn't bring back all those hours possibly 'wasted' in the dark of the movie theatre.

I could have gone on indefinitely writing film poems (Already I see that I've forgotten to include the pleasures of Jean Renoir, John Ford, Roberto Rossellini or even Kenneth Anger – with the latter director's *Inauguration of the Pleasure Dome* being for me a genuine act of magic, as artefact, that can't be re-interpreted with words.) Of course language cannot adequately convey the experience of film or music but that doesn't prevent us from attempting to critically make sense of what actually happens to us when a film proves to be so intense. Already I realise that I've contradicted myself. I chose not to convey the ritual magic of the Anger film but have included a poem for Dreyer's *Ordet* where a miracle (no special effects) occurs - a woman is brought back from the dead seemingly through the deliberately slow will-power of the film's direction.

My selections were conceived as prose poems. I didn't want them to be seen as solely eckphrastic pieces but a hybrid of forms. Prose poem, film review, autobiography, a 'letter' to a director, writer and sometimes an actor.

If you know and love my chosen films then I hope the poem adds to your enjoyment. And if you dislike the film or haven't seen it then hopefully my poem will make you seek the film out so as to disagree or experience it for the first time. It's an eclectic list beginning with Ingmar Bergman's *Persona* and ending with Terence Davies's *Distant Voices, Still Lives:* with SF, Horror, Japanese auteur cinema of the 50's, film noir, comedies, a Holocaust documentary and others sandwiched in between.

Here then are a handful of poems about the effect of the film image on me. How cinema enchanted and disturbed me to think a little differently about myself. They were a pleasure to write and I trust will give you pleasure to read.

For Roy and his Star Cinema

CONTENTS

The Cinephile Poems

THE CINEPHILE POEMS

PERSONA (1966)
directed by Ingmar Bergman

Psychoanalysis in a run-down art house / sex cinema. Aged 18 I didn't understand what this meant, Ingmar. You split open my physical, mental and spiritual defences. Alma and Elizabeth caressing each other's luminous faces: silenced actress and talkative nurse of vampirish moods. The psychiatrist's letter, a foot injured by shards of broken glass, self-immolation of a Buddhist monk on TV, a monologue, ravishment by the sea, the fights, babble of words: the merging of identities. Alma climaxing on nonsense speech, uttering, "A desperate perhaps." Then the projector broke down in the movie (not the theatre one whirring on that day) and a skeleton danced for the beginning and end of cinema. Speechless I escaped to a freezing street. I stared at the jigsaw image poster. It was snowing. Catharsis perhaps.

2001: A SPACE ODYSSEY (1968)
directed by Stanley Kubrick

For years I and other fans would ask What's Kubrick up to now? The waiting. The planning. The secrecy. The final result. *Stanley, Stanley give me direction do. I'm so spacey all for the love of you.* Your dawn of man's bone thrown into the sky –cutting me right to the quick. I'd never imagined waltzing in space before. And to gaze at that sentinel, reluctant to be anyone's partner. (Maybe the apes should have hugged it longer?) "Don't pull out my stops" cried HAL 9000 "You're about to really evolve." Not before a road-show intermission, an aborted rescue and a psychedelic storm of inner space. Exhausted from tripping I bussed-home wrapped in Cinerama 70mm. Next day I was re-born (no relaxation for a star-child.) Dragged out of my deep-freeze youth to realise one day I might end up old, alone dying in bed: faked objects of Western civilisation all around me. I broke a glass of water to imitate that smashed glass of astronaut wine: wondering if all my effort, in the face of entropy, added up to anything? Stanley, with Arthur C. Clarke, thought it just might or might not.

Your greatest adventure awaits you at...
2001
a space
odyssey
CASINO
CINERAMA

A MATTER OF LIFE AND DEATH (1946)
written and directed
by Michael Powell and Emeric Pressburger

No one has ever dramatised a brain seizure like you guys. An airman hallucinating on earth and its WW2 'heaven.' Pilot Peter Carter, so English a fighting poet. One moment in a three-strip Technicolor village, the next on a staircase to a monochrome beyond. Blaze of aircraft crashing down. A beach. Her cycling. You meet; grab the falling handlebars, embrace and kiss. Not some visionary sight of a nether world. Nor a surgeon spying the street with his camera obscura. Nor the French messenger who lost his head. Nor the smell of fried onions can change my mind: the idea of a sacrifice for love. June got her man. Peter got his woman. Emeric and you Michael got the film you wanted. AMOLAD determined my fantasy after-life. I was born premature three years later: taken out of my pram; nurtured in a cinema, entranced by black & white pearls with an option for wide screen rainbows. Hovering betwixt and between, knowing I'd never starve.

THE LADY VANISHES (1938)
directed by Alfred Hitchcock

Where did the lady vanish to, Alfred? They searched high and low on the train – even inside an illusionist's prop where pigeons flew out, white rabbits peered and the magician Doppo menaced with his knife. Margaret Lockwood's bang on the head, from a dropped flowerpot, became my bang on the head as I struggled to make the governess materialise. A dual concussion: the feeling I was going mad; Miss Froy never existed and Margaret and I needed a doctor. Then her name written on the compartment window; the train psychiatrist turning out to be a spy and the lady returned, bandaged on a stretcher. Your box of Alfred tricks conjured them up. Though a nun wearing high heels; the death of a lawyer and a final gunfight still conspired up your sleeve. *Miss Froy, Miss Froy I'll hum you a tune containing the secret code. English wit and international intrigue shall not grow old.* Many ladies vanished in many films yet to come (some I found, others not.) Yet only one, with welcoming arms, came back to the Foreign Office. After the film I rushed to the toilet and hit my head on its low lying ceiling. Dazed, wanting to go and lie down: re-live your perfect fluid dream – in spite of its test match ruined by a flood.

THE MAGNIFICENT AMBERSONS (1942)
directed by Orson Welles

"The magnificence of the Ambersons began in 1873. Their splendour lasted throughout all the years that saw their Midland town spread and darken into a city." Orson's bass-baritone voice intoning thwarted love, family decline and the birth of the motor car for the state of Indiana. *Mag-nificence!* phrased to capture the old making way for the new. Your imagery suffused with sadness for the passing of Amberson time, our times and my time watching you all in your darkening mansion. Agnes Morehead hysterical in the kitchen as George drank milk and gobbled shortcake to forget his social comeuppance. Mag-nificence, I'd repeat it to myself creating sacramental syllables. Why did you rush off to film a carnival in Brazil, Orson? Back home noisy preview audiences shot down your film as hard as the Japanese bombing of Pearl Harbour. Then came your Wise editor to butcher the ballroom scenes and replace your downbeat ending with that insanely happy surge. But let's not talk of tragic torsos but signs magnificent and resonant remains.

EYES WITHOUT A FACE (1959)
directed by Georges Franju

Christiane, of disfigured face, slowly ascends the staircase of the grey chateau. Your father Professor Genessier sweats and operates: amoral and determined. Scalpel and scissors cut away. A ring of forceps pins down the splayed face, waiting to be lifted up. Always failing to stay put: like the other faces of abducted women cracking and bleeding on every new owner. Christiane replaces her mask and descends to the cellar to stroke dumb beasts. Forty six years on I read a newspaper praising the first transplant. Mad doctors made respectable I thought. Today a face or two struggles to live: the glaring dead grafted onto scarred and scary messes. No real patient having the liberty of your heroine, Georges. Freeing chained dogs that ripped open her father's face; after a scalpel plunged deep into the neck of his assistant Louise; finally white doves uncaged to perch on her satin housecoat; crown her head, coo and fly off courageous into the night: ending an "anguish film." A "horror in homeopathic doses."

LOS OLVIDADOS (1954)
directed by Luis Bunuel

Bunuel, you were born to disregard Freud - never interpret our dreams only render them brutal, incomprehensible. Pedro's slow-motion filmed mother (how daintily she held up the sides of her nightdress.) The son asks "why no love and kisses?" She says her hands are tired from washing and reveals a lump of meat. Jaibo, Pedro's rival, appears from under the bed, grabbing at meat and timed to the sound of a thunderclap. Soon a legless dwarf will be thrown from his cart "One less. One less just like that and they will continue to drop. They should kill them before they were born" says a blind man, trying to molest a girl. Luis, your vision mellowed later in France for a bourgeois Michel Piccoli. Before this came an eye and an Andalusian razor. But this dead boy in a sack on a city waste dump. Where was he taken? I sat chilled in my seat, unable to cry: redemption gone missing: pushed outside of the frame.

BONNIE AND CLYDE (1967)
directed by Arthur Penn

I dispatched my parents to The Tunnel Road Picturedrome to see *Bonnie and Clyde.* What they found was *Gold Diggers of 1933* – a film within a film where Ginger Rogers sang, "We're in the money." Clyde sat in the back row, furious that they'd killed a man. Bonnie sighed. "If you boys want to talk why don't you all go outside?" Despite all the chatter in the 'flea-pit' my parents (who were never in any money) stuck with the stalls: watching kids rob banks and healthily shoot at rednecks. Arthur, I thought they'd hate your film but they loved it. That balletic massacre of an ending: how Bonnie and impotent Clyde writhed in orgasmic displeasure as bullets ripped through clothes and flesh. "It was horrible." said mother, unfazed. On that night screen violence, cocoa and toast brought me closer to Mum and Dad. I'd seen the film yonks before. My audience even younger, than the Barrow gang, with not a bloody-minded oldie in sight.

RIO BRAVO (1958)
directed by Howard Hawks

A bruised sheriff, an alcoholic deputy, a disabled man, a fast-gun teenager and a woman, once married to a gambler, honed their professionalism. Chance, Dude, Stumpy, Colorado and Feathers. Your men are Hawksian – just trying to complete a job of work. Your working woman the most emotionally professional of all. I was ten years old when Angie Dickinson became my screen mother. Nervy but confident. Dignified and disrespectful. Needing to know how long love would ever last. She chose John Wayne and kissed him before he could kiss her. I hadn't seen that in a western before. I never saw it at home. When they attacked the jail Feathers drank whiskey; dressed up fine and danced in the saloon and to allay my fears.

THE MALTESE FALCON (1941)
directed by John Huston

"You're good, you're very good." Sam Spade weighed up Miss Wonderly (her back facing him) as she poked the fire, lit a cigarette and fussed: allowing time for a further lie. Miss Wonderly became Brigid O'Shaughnessy to morph into Mary Astor for Humphrey Bogart to fall in love with. The falcon remained a leaden fake covering no diamonds and precious stones. Nothing but a MacGuffin: causing the fat man, the punk who shadowed and the one of perfumed handkerchiefs, to consider looking elsewhere, possibly Turkey. O'Shaughnessy confessed to shooting Miles, Sam's partner. Bogart, touching stardom, all gritted teeth and intense cold eyes, said he'd have a few sleepless nights but get over her. I went on holiday to Malta, finding a café called *The Falcon*. I sat there John, as your camera angles, direction and dialogue percolated through a waking dream. My Maltese coffee arriving too soon - luke warm and instant.

LA BELLE ET LA BETE (1946)
directed by Jean Cocteau

Your beauty and beast are the ones we most cherish: looking at mirrors, dreaming, awaiting transformation. Jean Marais was your lover off set, Monsieur Cocteau. Only in the shoot could Josette Day embrace the 'beast. 'Recoiling then approaching, ceremoniously taking hold of his paw: cupping water in her hand for a weeping Bête. In the castle grounds prowled a hairy repulsion with sad eyes; shot and killed by an arrow, changed into a spruced up prince who thinks Belle disapproves of because his face resembles her former boyfriend. Yes / No says a fickle Belle. "The first time I took you in my arms I was the beast. Are you happy?" "I'll have to get used to you." she replies. Back home from my first date I still glimpsed Belle shedding diamond tears for her dying father.

SPIONE (Spies, 1928)
directed by Fritz Lang

Fritz, you abandoned Dr.Mabuse for The Great Haghi, that super-criminal warning Sonia never to fall in love with her enemies. Murder, sabotage, stealing briefcases and international conspiracy are the only sure remit for a beautiful spy. That letter to the government - ridicule of the secret service had to end! Agent 326, now dressed as a bowler-hatted tramp, is briefed. He's just disarmed a double-agent with a smart camera (Such 007 gadgetry in 1928.) This oh so casual shrug of betrayal and sleaze. Spies getting everywhere. I exposed myself to a universe of evil. Inside the trap the nightmare went on forever. All those theorems, madness and fate. But your labyrinth held dark pleasure: shadows, design and abstract montage. Now we live in such a broken down spy-trap; watching each other more suspiciously than traitors in films in case romance sneaks in and disarms.

BOY (1969)
directed by Nagisa Oshima

"It's the end of Japan. We can't go any further."says the stepmother. "Grandmother won't want to see you" says the father. "We went to Hokkaido"says the son to the police. A journey of scam accidents right up to the snowy North. Boy learns how to fall; extorting money from drivers; faking bruises on arms, taught how long and when best to cry. A ten year old with a brother, only three, and a Mother pregnant with maybe another boy (snowed in) to hear the screech of brakes. A snowman, red Wellington boot and a dead girl. "Men from outer space will come to save the world" The boy assures his veteran father. As a child I too believed in cosmic forces. But a new wristwatch, that told you the date, and a family on the move wasn't for me. It belonged to Nagisa and his boy.

A CANTERBURY TALE (1944)
written and directed
by Michael Powell and Emeric Pressburger

An uptight sergeant driving a tank on the Canterbury Way. A London shop girl happy to be liberated on a tractor. An American soldier wanting to love the English and meet his buddy. In the blackout a Kent magistrate pours glue on young women's hair. The cinema organist longs to leave tanks alone and play in the cathedral. The American wood-cutter's anxious for his special girl. And the shop assistant weeps on opening her fiancée's moth-ridden caravan. Three pilgrims and a patriarchal avatar fated to find coins on the old Roman road, converge their blessings. Out of the church comes permission to play Bach or even Tin Pan Alley. Letters from the 'lost' girl are delivered to an exuberant buddy. A snobbish father breaks news of a tractor-woman's lover. Emeric and Michael's vision congregates in our heads a halo of technique - hiding, behind the sun. Transcendence can happen in the movies. But in life, the other side of the camera, I find it much less.

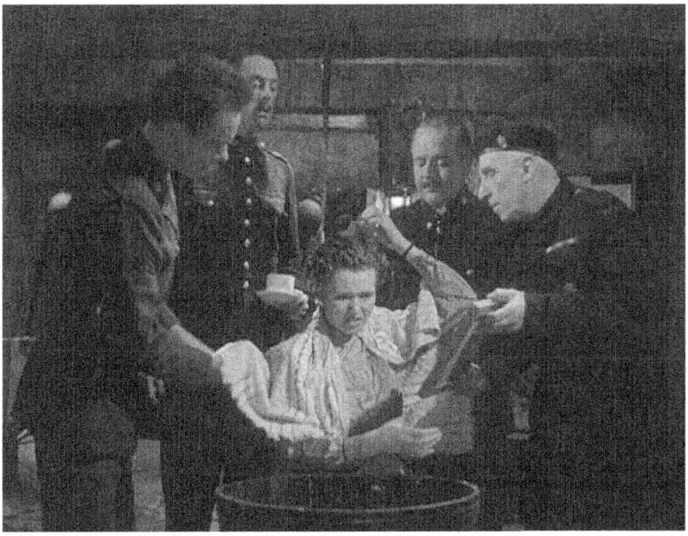

PICK UP ON SOUTH STREET (1953)
directed by Samuel Fuller

A necktie selling woman licked her pencil, informed the cops. Fifty dollars – last instalment on a Long Island burial plot. "I have to go on making a living so I could die." Plonked on her bed the shoes of a communist: gunning for a microfilm. The lady's head blown off. "Sweet Mademoiselle" loudly sings the record. For Sam Fuller life is terrible for 'dopey' looking agents. A three-time loser hangs out on a waterfront. A pickpocket throwing a beer to a sweating detective: dishing out bucks and hating routine. How on a summer day a thief unclipped the commie's girlfriend's bag in a subway train; groping behind tissues, makeup, ID, looking for money: scarcely registering the cops, the system, a dame's bruised face and transformative love so sticky on arrival. I never met a Red. Nearest I got was the SWP, gassy lager and an overdose of American imperialisms.

THE WIND (1928)
directed by Victor Sjostrom

A cattle buyer, a rancher and an old hired hand. Three suitors throwing sand at a woman in the wind: innocence sorely tested in Sweet Waters, Texas."The wind makes folks go crazy – especially women."declares the womaniser on the train. Lillian Gish knows all about craziness. An Indian ghost horse bucking through the sky. Old Norther spirit galloping into Lillian's tempest mind - kill this rapist, bury him quick in the sand. Victor's camera uncovers the face of a corpse. Gish clings to her husband rancher, long hair blowing free. The wind howls. "Mighty odd, if you kill a man in justice – the wind allers covers him." I still heard a March wind crying outside my flat after a TV commercial interrupted great gusts on the prairie.

SUMMER INTERLUDE (1951)
directed by Ingmar Bergman

Touring Sweden I wasn't disturbed by the colour of nature draining away – for summer will always be Bergman's in black and white. The ballerina wipes greasepaint off her face, removes false eyelashes and goes to the door to meet Dr. Coppelius who declares that life is futile. Her summer innocence has gone. Nothing makes much sense in the autumn. Returning from an island of crows where she stood by a handrail tackling a malign uncle who'd mailed the diary of her dead lover – the one who'd tasted wild strawberries. They'd laughed together and dived. He hit a rock and broke his back. This battered her heart and burnt mid-summer memories to a shrivel. The idyll of first love arose to choke her *Swan Lake.*

THE GOSPEL ACCORDING TO MATTHEW (1964)

directed by Pier Paolo Pasolini

What cinephile succour could I offer nuns and children enduring a film approved by the Pope? Timid souls fidget. One shields a little girl's eyes. Had the Vatican blown it? Good Friday's blistering gospel from a Marxist unbeliever."You will be hated by all, because you bear my name."Jesus rebukes, attacks, hectors and spits out his message; knifing the Pharisees, bursting open the moneylenders, stealing nets from fishermen. "Abandon family and friends" Jesus demands that their darkness can only receive his light. Armed with ecstasy and palms they dash towards Christ,
hand-held camera running as if a panther by their side. Then prowling in a cage behind the backs of soldiers, witnessing a rough-hewn Passion. Pasolini casting his own mother as the rejected Mary. Her lost Messiah, born to fight immaculate, returns to disobey: resurrected with a sword.

THE LIFE OF OHARU (1952)
directed by Kenji Mizoguchi
and acted by Kinuyo Tanaka

Her used body refutes men's status yet accepts its own sweat. All the crouching, swerving, running, stumbling and falling cannot break or save her now. Oharu's brief pleasure is not theirs slipping down from courtesan to concubine, shopkeeper, prostitute then labelled 'goblin cat'. The wife of a lord watches his concubine view a puppet show. Sold into a court of desire for an offspring. Oharu won't be bought as she sires a son that's pulled from her arms. Slapped like a fish on a chopping board she flops, despising law and order. When old they rent her a gaudy dress and underwear but Oharu returns to claw and hiss. Each movement of Ohura's hand, touching her veil, cries out disdain, holding intact
a huge sad grace. They'll not abuse what's deepened inside. She fainted inside me, shaming us all for our looking on. I retreated from the screen.

UGETSU MONOGATARI (1953)
directed by Kenji Mizoguchi

Sunlight, enchantment, erotic truces and Lady Wakasa appear as a potter brings his merchandise to the market, over-reaching for a dream bigger than his family. A deceased princess lambent in a ruined house tempts her man and artisan to love firm and long. Ambition, money, delusion and a civil war reside as a mother with child, tied to her back, is struck by a spear to totter on the path made cruel and tender for all to view. Miyaki reappears to sew her husband's kimono; become a domestic ghost united with Genjuro who will now create pots more beautiful than before when he lost his soul to the kiln, greed keeping its fire alight. Once I watched my mother mend a pair of trousers and argue with father till each forgiving stitch was outed. Now Mizoguchi's camera tracks down all evil spirits intent on destroying fired earthenware and any belief in the humility of sewing.

SANSHO DAYU (1954)
directed by Kenji Mizoguchi

Zu-shio An-ju, Zu-shio An-ju, Zu-shio An-ju, Zu-shio An-ju. Cry of an aristocratic woman spanning time and space. Why were Tamaki and her children sold into slavery? Wrenched apart, dispatched to torments: sold for a legend. Her wail turned into a song composed of loss, fire and water learnt by a weaver in the camp, invoking the memory and heart of sister and brother. *Zu-shio An-ju, Zu-shio An-ju.* Names as telepathy cutting deep into birdsong woods, escaping through a gate, rippling on the lake of the drowned, capturing that most cruel of stewards, angering the state, inciting rebellion and demanding freedom for all slaves. A parallel fate was the savage breaking of Tamaki's tendon, her blindness, chanting and collection of mute seaweed: asking to be banished by the embrace of mother and son. And a mythic song to be silenced by father's mercy, both real and mystical, approaching the edge of the seashore. It hurts to see characters in a story suffer too much. I wanted to rescue this family from a life of beautiful compositions.

THE SPIRAL STAIRCASE (1946)
directed by Robert Siodmak

In the hotel an eye watched at the back of a wardrobe till a body blacked out, hands clawing at strangled air. *Babies in arms are not permitted* read the bare regulation. Held tight by mother I was bundled in to disturb the rules of their dark. If she'd turned for a second, made me choke on projected light then the sound of a theremin and an old dark house would have recharged their menace, fixed me about-face in the Cameo cinema where a New England psychopath killed the weak and unnecessary. A mute examined herself in a mirror: mouth blotted away by his stare. She gathered terror into a scream to break open her voice on the phone for the doctor with a pony, trap and loving eye to rescue her from the storm - body on a staircase, iodine for an invalid, a wronged man, a smashed window, the dead girl dumped in the cellar: his flickering, re-emerging to scrape at her throat.

THE ADVENTURES OF ROBINSON CRUSOE
(1952)
directed by Luis Bunuel

This thirsty son who went to sea was quickly shipwrecked; hallucinating his father wasting water by scrubbing a pig. Bunuel sipped much Hungarian red directing his Crusoe who drank rum and imagined harmonising with shipmates: only to sob long and hard when they suddenly vanished. Father drowned and his dog Rex died in the pouring rain. When Crusoe shouted psalm 132 and heard his echo taunt Robinson: all he'd left to master were insects to feed unleavened bread or let them devour one another. After 18 years came Friday, ignorant of making a footprint, who put on a woman's dress, wore a necklace of gold coins and waved his sword. With no hint of desire they debated, hunted and thrived as master and slave on a godless island forgotten by the devil. I returned to the book to discover a hoarding Crusoe who couldn't befriend this screen Crusoe singing to his crops of Eastman-colour stock.

© picture-alliance/Mary Evans Picture Library

THE INCREDIBLE SHRINKING MAN (1957)
directed by Jack Arnold.

I once dreamt of becoming smaller and smaller; my trousers fell down and the world ignored me so how could I possibly help an average man, shrinking in suburbia, on a black and white film? That insecticide spray and radioactive mist meant disaster for you Robert Scott Carey in our world of competing giants: forced to live in a doll's house, then a match box. They thought a cat named Butch ate tiny Bob but no one dissected the cat to find out. He'd fallen into the cellar where he rescued cheese from a mousetrap, clung to a pencil to survive a flood and with a nail killed a spider so as to eat stale cake; all the while hoping his wife would come. But she drove away with Bob's brother, taller than her. When the cake crumbled in your hand you gave up old hunter instincts. The circle of the incredibly small and incredibly vast consoled. Such infinity of nature and God's plan, on your side, for further shrinkage, driving every molecule with a greater urge to exist.

MESA OF LOST WOMEN (1953)
directed by Ron Ormond and Herbert Tevos

"Perhaps they're only elusive images produced by roasting the optic nerve." No, film narrator. They really are inept actors sleepwalking through a trashy movie. Simply (?) transfer the pituitary gland of a beautiful woman onto a tarantula and make it grow as large as a human being, plant its spider growth hormone into the girl, remembering to change her name to Tarentella, and she will survive for hundreds and hundreds of years. "The amazing durability of my creations." exclaims the scientist on the mesa, full of male dwarves and busty women, in a Mexican desert. However when Tarentella performed the Tarantula Dance, wearing a sexy halter-top, in that sleazy dive, her hand raised, with two fingers pointing down, as if to sting you, I forgave this cinematic atrocity, bought in a bargain basement, almost everything. She was shot dead and quickly returned to life: idiocy was piled upon idiocy. My brain melted. Clinging to her mesa blonde colleague and spider (wire controlled) I staggered down poverty row to enter its Death-Site Asylum.

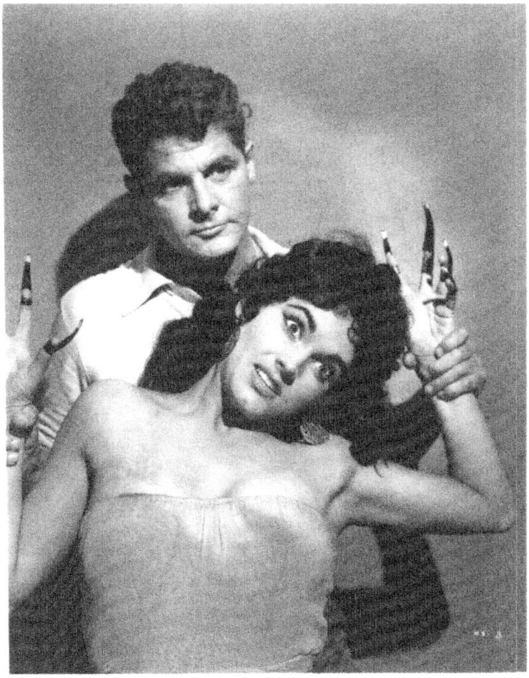

IT (1927)
directed by Clarence Badger
and acted by Clara Bow

Have you got IT? You must have. Don't ever be it-less. Clara had it – canyons of bounce, eyeing up the boss: charisma, with red hair, giving audiences the triple look. First for "the love sick dames." Second, those horny guys. Third, old ladies who coughed and forgave the shocks as she lingered, lusted, then calibrated box-office innocence. Sprawling across an executive desk, pouting and dancing at the Ritz or devouring her burger and man on Coney Island. To hell with the boss's blonde. This flapper will have him. A shop assistant who can't read a fancy French menu says "Gimme the same as you but for love makin' I translate." I once served long hours in shops finding no Clara Bows either side of the counter: went to the movies after work, sat through every new helping of female IT sensing Ms Bow hangin' around, urging all to desire then laugh em' out loud.

SECRET BEYOND THE DOOR (1947)
directed by Fritz Lang

More than enough Freudianisms to have delighted Sigmund: keys, doors, corridors, lilacs, a stone lion spouting water, wax cut from a candlestick, a duellist's knife, church bells and a secretary's long-held pretence of a scarred face bristle in the light and shadow of an obsessed husband who collects and furnishes rooms, aching from murders, committed by others, then pushes away any suggestion that he has a Bluebeard complex to one day confront. Joan Bennet knew something was up, on brushing her hair two hundred times, as the door handle rattled, then checked to find Michael Redgrave wasn't there. I watched them all on TV that wet afternoon: Lang's gothic power rupturing the schedules. The music welled up on the final credits and an actor's role was listed as the Intellectual Sub-Deb. A scene stealer, questioning the collector on his tour of the house, should have said "Analysts will come to fall in love with the movie delirium that I've been cast in."

WHITE HEAT (1949)
directed by Raoul Walsh
and acted by James Cagney

A gang member scalded by steam from the mail train then bandaged up and left to die waiting for the Doc. Now if ever I burn myself badly at my kitchen stove indifference will return in the form of Arthur Cody Jarret snarling from his pain and lust in mother's open arms till his girlfriend enters, spits out her gum and demands a fur coat, shivering treacherously in their hide-out. Those 'tops' of Jarret's world kept peaking in madness; a routine killing whilst gnawing away on a chicken leg, 'epilepsy' as a manic protest in a prison dining hall and that firing of your gun at the chemical storage tank exploding with a blast to ape your psychotic torment and meltdown audiences for an atomic age. "All I ever had was Ma." She was the gang's engineer. Her son the ruthless driver despising the rest: plagued by headaches from hell and incurably in love with Mom, especially when she was shot by Cody's gal. All the punk gangsters, that came after Cagney, merely lit the fuse he'd already planted in our brains.

WITCHFINDER GENERAL (1968)
directed by Michael Reeves

A scream trapped inside a pastoral East Anglia. Violence is now contagious for all the landscape. Beauty and horror cleave the trees, grass, river even sunlight. Betwixt the mob, priests, witches, and Cromwell's further intentions, a soldier and his wife are accused of conversing with the devil - a black cat and a stoat, those invisible familiars. World out of joint. Rebellious. Pursuing idolaters. Many are tortured, drowned and cast into the fire. A hard evil questions all: hot iron branding the flesh with the mad belief that God wills all this. The Hopkins general is caught and struck down, by an axe that refuses to stop. "You took him away from me!" roars the Roundhead. Whilst the scream of his girl Sarah carries on and on; freezing the end titles to lodge inside my head. Next day I walked past the cinema, not the desecrated church, where she was angrily wed.

THE TIME MACHINE (1960)
directed by George Pal

It is New Year's Eve 1899 and we shall travel in time to the year 802,701; stopping off at 1917, 1940 and 1966 to sample their wars." He has all the time in the world." declares Filby, the botanist friend of time traveller H. George Wells who'll return to Weena the childlike woman to be woken again from her docile existence. In 802,701 the Eloi played in the sun, ignored old books, crumbling to dust, and metal rings you could spin to speak of conflict and disaster; the Morlocks took all the blonde Elois calmly underground to eat them up, making the cruel point that a species must always grow and develop. Yet if George had taken time out to speed to the year 635,427,810 then Mother Earth, now a dying wasteland, would have filled him with dread. All this was filmed in 1960 when I, an eleven year old, desired a time machine and futures to play with: abandon all my dead schooling, stay alive, curious and unbound.

THE NIGHT OF THE HUNTER (1954)
directed by Charles Laughton

I witnessed a dark fairy tale through the changing of the reels on a 16m projector: young, drinking wine, after a birthday party, came our Southern treat: a vision of West Virginia horror. When Willa found the flick-knife in the preacher's pocket and warmly said, "Men!" you knew that she was doomed. The priestly husband tilted back his head, raised up an arm to the window of the high-gabled bedroom as if to sing an aria for the Devil, his legal employer. The message was the falling blade: then a drowned wife, hair streaming with the seaweed, sat upright in her Model T. Auto. The children will endure and survive the hunter (Death leaning on the foolish and good.) Escaping down the river watched by a frog, owl, rabbits, and us, through a spider's web. Never seeming to sleep he chases you on horseback. A shotgun's fired. When arrested a stepson beats his sister's doll against the killer's chest bursting out the stuffed dollar bills so craved. Hands tattooed with Harry's Love and Hate; once gripped tight for a monster's contest, now helpless, as lambs, handcuffed to the reverend wolf.

MARNIE (1964)
directed by Alfred Hitchcock

"Pulling her skirt down over her knees as if they were a national treasure. And then she robbed me." Mr. Strutt knew best, Marnie. He employed a thief, cheat and liar without ever asking for references. "Oh, that one. The brunette with the legs." Caught with Mark inside his office, during a thunder storm, by a watched race track, within a boat's cabin and floating in a pool as red flooded the screen: from ink spilt on a blouse to blood on that poker from beating the head of a sailor. "Marnie, you're achin' my leg." Mother taking her newly blonde daughter to task for desiring men. "I don't like him to kiss me. Make him go, Momma!" A thief collapsing then speaking, in a child's voice, about all her desperate Marnies: money, sex, attention and Mrs Edgar's love not far behind. Needs now paraded for the Hitchcockian gaze. Once in France I watched *Marnie* dubbed on TV without sub-titles: undergoing, with my girlfriend, messed up by her mother, further anxieties.

VIVRE SA VIE (1964)
directed by Jean Luc-Godard

Faces are hidden, save for reflections out of focus: camera eavesdropping on the backs of two heads. In a wintry Paris Nana talks to Paul of how to end this thing called a relationship. Her soul is confined in a coffee bar until Godard allows Anna Karina to become his Nana crying at everyone's *Jeanne D'arc,* and suffering as Falconetti in a cinema: being questioned and judged. Karina's stark tableaux in twelve parts – a journey through "bad faith", prostitution, B-picture crooks, and a left-bank philosopher. With a close-up purity of face Nana looked at me and said, "I want to be someone else." Not this actress in her husband's film. "I'm responsible for my life." But did Nana think that as she joyfully danced and sang in a bar or just before she was shot dead by a pimp on the street? At eighteen I embraced all things existential, adopting Karina to face the indifference of the world.

RECORD D
DANNY
DOU
DU GE
EN SCOPE
LES PLU
ARTISTES
AMO
CELE
EN SCOPE
VARIETES
L'ARNAQUEUR
EN CINEMASCOPE

NIGHT AND FOG (1956)
directed by Alain Resnais
and written by Jean Cayrol

In autumn light, developed as if the grain of film stock, I walked the few kilometres from Auschwitz to Birkenau discovering a railway track loosely handcuffed by weeds: the end of a journey begun in your document shadowing my footsteps; its camera tracking through deserted huts, latrines and crematorium. Incinerator, cold in my presence, burns raw inside the heart: hard to touch rust and iron or even recoil from celluloid. Himmler greets technicians. "We must destroy but productively." Gold teeth extracted. Human heads in barrels. Skulls arranged on the ground. Godard told us to show this film on television - for ever. And now, on ever newer screens: nights follow days with fogs in constant pursuit.

IT HAPPENED HERE (1964)
directed by Kevin Brownlow and Andrew Mollo

It happened once again: moving to London in 1980, seeing 14 Belsize Square, NW3 (Now Garden Flat 16a) filmed in 1964, to be crushed by an imaginary 1945. I stood outside the long-gone doctor's surgery, remembering the actor inside who'd said that fascism could only be defeated by the use of fascist methods. Pauline recoiled: a nurse who'd escaped a massacre by the partisans; trying to keep active, apolitical: joined Immediate Action Operations and came to hate both their salute and solutions – the staff rest-room with racists talking of the weak and unnecessary and the sleepy country hospital where she was given a needle to prick the disease of 'worn-out' workers from the Eastern front. Then captured by partisans slaughtering German soldiers in a field: asked to help wounded rebels as the rat-tat-tat-tat-tat of the others continued. In the city a cosy Englishness still occupied the heads of citizens: shoes cleaned, buses driven, trains departing, an army chatting up the London girls, kids doing a cheeky goose-step, a soldier photographing his mates outside the Albert Hall: with flaming torches a Nazi anthem was sung by a gang, so solidly British, for their murdered comrade: with widow and son now to be nursed by a comfortable Reich.

PINA (2011)
directed by Wim Wenders
and choreographed by Pina Bausch

Dancing on a traffic island for cars and buses speeding by: a train passes. Dancing in the country. It's Autumn. She falls. He catches her. She falls. He catches her. *Don't forget you have to scare me.* Women leaping onto men joyfully leaning back on their chairs. Performing solo by a rock with water splashing followed by dirt shovelled over your body. *You have to get crazier to dance.* Female, on ballerina points, by a power station. Boggie Woogie on the dance floor. Retreat. Advance. A red dress offered to the chosen one in the sacrificial part of Stravinsky's Rite. *Your fragility is also your strength.* And those final dancers, like children, in equilibrium, fists closed and shaking over their jacket lapels, dress tops; a line moving to Louis Armstrong's trumpet, on a hill top, at dusk, affirming, sublime. *Dance for love.* I changed my mind about being Gene Kelly or Fred Astaire as those bodies of Bausch, in 3D grace, expanded my vision through time and space.

CITY LIGHTS (1931)
directed by Charles Chaplin

"You?" says the former blind girl, now an all-seeing florist. A tentative Chaplin nods his head. "You can see me now?" (He'd been a swanky destitute playing at being wealthy.) Girl nods back – widening the gulf, freezing the moment. he gives a rose to a tramp, which he puts in his mouth; smiling with his longing, her waiting: silent deception and a live orchestra sprung for tragedy. My partner cried. She was glad to have seen the film, especially with me. I smiled more at ease; having nothing to say or prove, no one to manipulate, nor any need to suffer the burden of being a universal tramp.

ORDET (The Word, 1955)
directed by Carl Theodor Dreyer

One hundred and fourteen shots – long takes, tracks, pans and wipes: on average measuring ninety seconds. A slow journey to resurrection. Everyone talks much, not giving direct eye contact: distracted and waiting for the word to be spoken: a conflict of love, madness and faith for a Jutland family at their farmhouse. A kitchen glowing with utensils, constant drinking of coffee, and the opening and closing of doors by a priest and doctor. That holy fool, convinced he was Christ, now calmed down, assisted by a child, to bring Mother, who died in childbirth, back from the dead. All that spent passion, anguish and grief. All that talk about the truth of miracles. And then she rises up from her coffin; to kiss and mouth her husband's cheek, hungry for him and her baby (He's told her it now lives in the house of God.) I felt things supernatural, coursing through my body. When I walked along a London street that mother cried "life" to the polluted air and drowned the traffic noise.

L'AVVENTURA (1960)
Directed by Michelangelo Antonioni

A rich Italian party: bodies, looks, gestures, an island, rocks, the sea, a church, a piazza and a rooftop holding on to a continual ache in a exquisite design of loneliness.Anna went missing on the island. She was already about to vanish; made invisible by her friends' boredom. Her body never found. No one's ever found. The camera as Anna's ghost watching others failing to see her or themselves. Claudia and Sandro lie kissing in a field as a train passes giving meaning, or maybe nothing at all to their passion. Do you love me? Why do you love me? What do I need from you? Who am I? Claudia tenderly placing her hand on the back of Sandro's head, as he sits on a bench. Not to forgive his infidelity. Nor show pity...yet. I let the film fall into my mind, validate my melancholy, unable or unwilling to deflect this other time and place.

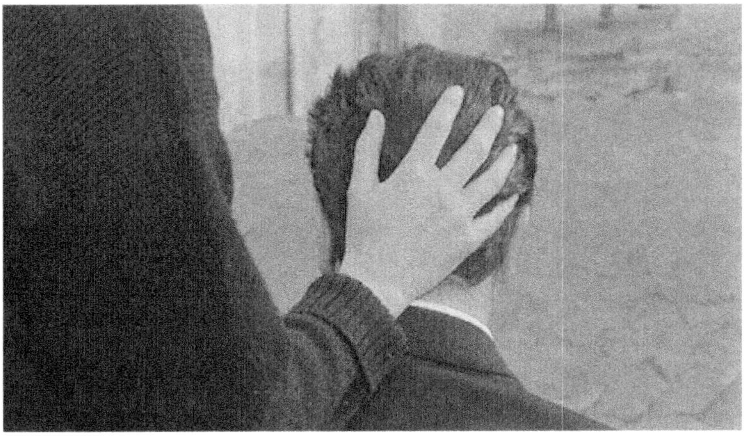

DISTANT VOICES, STILL LIVES (1988)
directed by Terence Davies

"We shall not gather by the river but in the beautiful pub. We'll have a sing-song to praise, then quickly batter down our bringing up. Our religion's Catholic yet we prefer beer and candles to wine with that brute our father in the cellar." Two daughters fighting against the blows of a broom. A son conscripted to the army; returning to swear, light a fag, marry and escape. Lives desiring to escape tyranny. *If you knew Susie. Buttons and Bows. Taking a chance on love.* Voices joined with neighbours over an ale-drenched piano. This was their opera, romance, ballad and M.G.M. musical. Ceremony. Ritual. Cry of the camera. Cutting down of ambition. *I wanna be around to pick up the pieces when somebody breaks your heart.* A family in time and memory. A street's existence under the stars. I heard my dead brother crooning loud and raw. I caught myself, a young shipping clerk, in a Liverpool long vacated: all its celebrations eclipsed by time.

AFTERWORD

I didn't realise it then but the genesis of *The Cinephile Poems* was twenty four years ago in my unpublished novel, *Spiral Movie.* It's the semi-autobiographical story of a working class boy growing up in Toxteth, Liverpool 8 and falling under the spell of going to the cinema. I showed chapters to friends (some were writers others not) and mailed the manuscript to publishers who returned it with handwritten notes saying I enjoyed this but it's not for us. One publisher did accept *Spiral Movie* but wanted me to contribute £7000 to fund the cost of launching a novelist. I declined, put my book away and turned to scriptwriting and short stories.

Eight years ago I re-read *Spiral Movie* and felt that a great deal of it wasn't really working. David Thomson's book *Suspects* and moments in Terence Davies's film *The Long Day Closes* had been a background influence. Yet structurally I felt their work was much stronger than mine. I didn't want to attempt another re-write so I chopped up my material and inserted the autobiographical bits into blogs on my Wordpress site. alanprice69

By this time I'd returned to writing poetry. My first poetry collection *Outfoxing Hyenas* had been published and I was working on a pamphlet. A few film-related poems are in *Outfoxing Hyenas* and subsequent books. The idea of a book of purely film poems was floating around, hence eventually came *The Cinephile Poems.*

I've gone and included a short extract from the first chapter of *Spiral Movie* and a blog essay on three influential films of my childhood and adolescence. They've been slightly revised and I am happy about that. With *Persona* and *The Spiral Staircase* there's some repetition of material yet I hope it proves interesting to see how prose poems evolved out of them. As for the Beatles' film *A Hard Day's Night* well it didn't need a poem, simply watch and listen to its captivating music and lyrics. I couldn't ever compete with that happiness.

THE SPIRAL MOVIE

THE SPIRAL MOVIE

Chapter 1

Martin was being watched by a great eye.

It wasn't his mother's eye. Hers were blue green and awake.

It wasn't his father's eye. His were brown and shut in sleep.

Did the eye belong to the boy? A cyclopic force projecting itself outside of him? No. Martin had no sense of investigating himself. He couldn't understand one of his infant eyes, out there, locked onto a ring-eyed forehead. Looking over him, through him, after him.

The eye was human, that much he did know: though its gaze seemed able to penetrate the rock of a mountain this was no angry Cyclops but a watching thing in itself whose purpose was to look you over. Weigh up everything. See what was needed. The eye's power easily dwarfed the authority of Martin's parents and his threatened innocence, on that day or maybe night.

The sheen of the eyeball was excited, ravenous to observe: catch all the people gathered in a darkened place. This would be a secret ceremony for the worship of the eye. And everyone was compelled to look.

A blink of its eyelash and Martin would have been lost, scooped into the iris and helplessly inverted, all his little secrets raced along an optic nerve to a brain he did not, could not know. The fate of the room's other watchers didn't concern the child. He only knew that they shouldn't be there, ought not to be looking at his great eye.

Mother had caused these people to stand up as she nervously made for her seat. There was a ripple of complaint, louder protests, shuffling and the slam of hard seats. She was late for the ritual.

Gripped by mother Martin was allowed these first perceptions of what lay in 'the cave.' Huge shadows were switched on and thrown up on its wall. The joy and terror of machine light. Such a strange conjured world. Appearances. What was real? What was false?

He looked anxiously at Mother. Her breast, neck, face and eye. All that seemed secure was eclipsed. For she too was entranced, subjugated by the eye thing.

Martin looked backwards and saw a long beam of light coming from a slot in the wall. His tiny hand wanted to grab its dust, gobble it up. Yet that would have entailed a miraculous flight from his mother's khaki overcoat, going over the heads of the watchers and diving into the intense light.

Martin heard music and sounds. A woman walked up an old staircase lit by gaslight. Routinely. Innocently. Not yet benighted. She stopped and began to address a large mirror hinged to a wall. It was obvious that she was pretending to talk, mimic speech. That she was dumb.

The great eye was thrilled by this young mute. She'd stepped into a lascivious trap. A misty blur stole over the woman's face to erase her mouth. No vocal chords to pretend a voice. No hole in the face to gesticulate a scream – if that's what she wanted. She couldn't rub off the horrid blur. She was dumbstruck and possibly about to die.

The frenzied eye began to mouth her.

The child wanted to shout beware but he'd no language.

The eye and blur retreated to the staircase.

Who would save her?

The unseen woman.

Yes.

She cried Helen! before a flash of darkness and her appearance. Martin glanced at Mother. Tears ran down her face as Martin experienced his first mental fall, being caught inside the 'desirable' mechanism of watching. Lit up with the glow of gazing. Out there the projected gaze formed other pressing faces in this compelling dream, controlling image, looking glass, cinema.

Martin was told he was only two when his mother took him to see The Spiral Staircase. He was sneaked in to the Cameo cinema, in Liverpool, on a rainy afternoon. Mother remembered this clearly for after ten minutes she had to leave on account of a heavy cold.

Two years previous the cinema experienced the shooting of the manager and his assistant by a gunman who escaped with the day's takings of fifty pounds. That crime was solved for they quickly caught the man. But Martin's film ritual was interrupted.

No. Suspended.

For thirty eight years that close-up of the eye of a homicidal killer hovered (accompanied by the electronic oscillations of a Theremin.) Martin never discovered the film murderer's identity or what happened to Helen. In fact he didn't see the film all the way through until 1987 one year before his father died.

On late night TV the great eye peered back like an unwelcome guest. "I know you. Know who you really are. There's no room for imperfection in the world! "it said. Martin was startled. Fear, conscience and guarded reason demanded that he watch all of *The Spiral Staircase* and solve the mystery. Yet the delay between the heroine's dumbness and the first sounds she uttered, at the end of the movie, was far greater than ninety minutes of screen time.

It was possibly more than half Martin's life.

It was the distance between the estrangement of his parents' marriage and mad figures manoeuvring on a screen. And the guilt of those figures that long ago had exacerbated Mother's cold in a draughty cinema: perhaps if she'd stayed the course then the boy who'd have been less frightened by the whole film. That is it was the very interruption of his film-watching that most disturbed Martin. A glimpse of unexplained terror lingered.

Mother had introduced Martin to cinema magic but didn't accept responsibility for the fact. In this public but also private world Martin grew up collecting images to trade with friends and lovers.

The New England murderer of Robert Siodmak's forties film noir was the boy's first celluloid visitor: a predator who prowled through turn of the century gothic rooms. Further strange persons came and knocked on Martin's door. The big eye ushered in more films and dream states than he could have ever imagined.

Martin learnt to place his hand against the screen and trace things and people as they emerged, superimposed themselves, ran alongside of him, in the present, and then vanished. This wasn't an attempt to explain his past fifty years but describe what occurred during the big fade out and fade in.

Before the eye. After the eye. Or even minus the eye.

Closing his eyes wasn't an option.

He had to be made to see.

THREE FILMS THAT SHAPED ME

THREE FILMS THAT SHAPED ME

Martin Scorsese has said of Visconti's *The Leopard* that "It is one of the films I live by." In his documentary, *My Voyage to Italy* Scorsese gives us an autobiographical account of why neo-realism, mattered to him whilst growing up. The films of De Sica, Visconti, Rossellini and later on Antonioni, Pasolini and Fellini, coloured his youth and helped to form his career as a filmmaker.

Here are three films that I lived with, rather than by, that influenced my childhood and adolescence.

THE SPIRAL STAIRCASE

An enormous close-up of the eye of a New England killer, who champions beauty, and then undertakes to rid the world of handicapped or disfigured women what I was exposed to as a young baby, with my mother. *The Spiral Staircase* was showing at the Cameo cinema in Liverpool in 1950. The building, formerly a church, had a neon sign over a stained glass window. Much lower down it bore that cinema warning of the fifties, "Babies, in arms, not admitted" (A message blithely ignored by the manager, who needed a bigger audience for the matinees.)

My mother got in and held me very tight as a huge close-up of a malevolent eye feverishly watched her and heroine Dorothy McGuire. I've no idea if my face was directed towards the screen or whether it was pressed against my mother's breast. Years later she told me that she often slipped into The Cameo in the afternoon, and that *The Spiral Staircase* really was one of those films she'd let me 'see.' Did I cry because I actually witnessed that eye? Or did I only cry because I was hungry? I like to think I absorbed the power of that black and white eye and was none the worse for it.

I can't claim *The Spiral Staircase* to be the first film I properly saw (The first was *Devil Girl from Mars,* watched at the age of six all the way through.) Yet that primal celluloid eye was the first film image, hanging around in the dark, wanting to pull me in.

An intriguing prequel to all this was that 16 days after my birth, on the 19th March 1949, the cinema manager, and his assistant, were shot by a gunman who escaped with the days takings of £50. A real murder occurring at the box office. A year later a mother and her baby where watching murders on screen in a church converted into a cinema. Cinema proved to be far more important than religion. Cinephilia becomes my secular gospel.

A HARD DAY'S NIGHT

That final clashing Beatle music chord and then the fire-doors of the Odeon cinema, in London Road, Liverpool, were opened freeing hoards of children to greet the July sunshine. I ran on through the streets, all the way back home, two miles away.

'Rarely, rarely comest thou, spirit of delight" said Shelley in one of his poems. Adrenalin high I narrowly missed hitting traffic and people; dazed with the belief and confidence that I could do anything. Happiness enveloped me that evening. My staid parents shook their heads. I couldn't eat my meal; only devour the food of liberating Beatle songs playing in my head.

A Hard Day's Night was not so much a pop musical as a teenage-music fix. I was high on the force of its blasting optimism. Richard Lester's film is a plot-redundant account of Beatlemania in 1964, when the Beatles were at their youthful harmonic peak. The Beatles opened up the door to popular music; announcing that if we four guys, from Liverpool, could make it then anyone could. The sixties was a more innocent time, when optimism wasn't a discredited word and the young could be pro-actively idealistic. Whether *A Hard Day's Night* is a great film, or not, is irrelevant. It has a joy that makes me feel good to be alive.

PERSONA

1967 – four years later. Different weather and a very different film. A chilly December afternoon. I'd just come out of Liverpool's Jacey Film Theatre cinema. As I walked through the falling snow I was thoughtful and reflective yet at the same time excited and disturbed by what I'd just sat through. Nothing had prepared me for the experience of Bergman's *Persona* - this self-examination of two women, a nurse (with a lot to say) and an actress (with nothing to say.) The tension of their relationship, resulting in the merging of each others personality, left me emotionally exhausted. *Persona* gave me an experience akin to psychotherapy.

Aged seventeen and on the verge of adulthood, the film had thrown so much in doubt. Can we ever fully communicate with one another? How intact is human personality? Can it be broken down so easily and re-cast? Do we have to retreat inside ourselves to escape the injustice of the world? Or do we make a stand and cry out? What is sexual identity? An often fierce battle between nurse and patient. What was that really all about? Why did their femininity matter to me?

Persona is also an erotic film. Liv Ullman and Bibi Anderson were exciting and sensual, Scandinavian actresses of great beauty and intelligence. *Persona's* imagery flooded my head. It contains some of the most powerful close-ups, in all cinema, conveying not simply the beauty and mystery of the human face, but abstractions and ideas about the human condition so bonded to the flesh and spirit.

Persona is a profound, if bleak experience. Yet it contains, as film critic Robin Wood wrote, in his book on Ingmar Bergman, 'a desperate perhaps.' As an impressionable teenager, lured by the arts, that 'perhaps' was what I also took from this ruthlessly honest and courageous film. Every time I see *Persona* nothing remains stable, comfortable or fixed. Female and male identity are in flux, creating a dynamic of silence and speech stretching you to the limits and at the same time questioning the means by which cinema can engage with mind, body and the interface of the political / social order of the world.

ACKNOWLEDGEMENTS

Acknowledgements: Some of these poems have been published in *The High Window, The French Literary Review, London Grip, The Wednesday, The Recusant, Bakings* and *The Tokyo Poetry Journal.*

THE HIGH WINDOW

The following collections are also available from our website, where further information will be found:
thehighwindowpress.com

A Slow Blues, New and Selected Poems
by David Cooke
Angles & Visions by Anthony Costello
The Emigrant's Farewell by James W. Wood
Four American Poets edited by Anthony Costello
Dust by Bethany W. Pope
From Inside by Anthony Howell
The Edge of Seeing by John Duffy
End Phrase by Mario Susko
Bloody, proud and murderous men, adulterers and enemies of God
by Steve Ely
Bare Bones by Norton Hodges
Wounded Light by James Russell
Bone Antler Stone by Tim Miller
Wardrobe Blues for a Japanese Lady by Alan Price
Trodden Before by Patricia McCarthy
Janky Tuk Tuks by Wendy Holborow
Cradle of Bones by Frances Sackett
Of Course, the Yellow Cab by Ken Champion
Forms of Exile: Selected Poems of Marina Tsvetaeva
translated by Belinda Cooke
West South North North South East by Daniel Bennett
Surfaces by Michael Lesher
Man Walking on Water with Tie Askew
by Margaret Wilmott

Songs of Realisation by Anthony Howell
Building a Kingdom,
New and Selected Poems 1989-2019
by James W. Wood
The Unmaking by Tim O'Leary
Out of the Blue, Selected Poems by Wendy Klein
Daylight of Seagulls by Alice Allen
Man at the Ice House by Alison Mace
Empire of Eden by Tom Laichas
Visiting Hours by Kitty Coles
Is Anyone There? by Martin Zarrop
The Trio Confessions by Alan Price
Before Silence, a year's haiku by Michel Onfray
translated by Helen May Williams
Stem by Belinda Cooke
Slippage, Poems 2013-2018
by David Cooke
Walking Away, New and Selected Poems
by Shaun Traynor
The Leading Question by Roger Elkin
Of Gardens and Witches, a herbal
The Boycott by Sally Michaelson
Silver Samovar by Jenny McRobert
Ancient Modern by Timothy Dodd
Shepherd's Warning by Mervyn Linford
Finding My Footprints by David Cooke
Mollusc by Mark Totterdell
Invention of Reality by Anthony Howell
Workwear by Carla D'Antonio Scarano

Printed in Great Britain
by Amazon

17615841R00068